You Did It Where?
The Strangest Places People
Have Sex

by
Brad Tassell

illustrations by
Adam Stivers

Llessat Publishing
Evansville, IN

YOU DID IT WHERE?
The Strangest Places People Have Sex.

Llessat Publishing
3527 Elmridge
Evansville, IN 47711

International Standard Book Number: 0-89708-215-X

Library of Congress Catalog Number: 94-09091

First Printing, April 1994

97 96 95 94   1 2 3 4 5 6 7 8 9

INTRODUCTION

People are finding in the nineties that monogamy is the only alternative to celibacy. But monogamy doesn't have to mean monotony. The adventurous modern couple is cutting out all other partners and adding atmosphere and suspense to their sexual menu.

I have never seen people get more excited at my shows than when I started asking audience members to fill out my questionnaires on strange sex places. They loved talking about it, and you will love reading about the strangest of the strange.

The acts described in this book are all alleged to be true by the people who participated. I sure don't recommend some of the more dangerous stunts, but you will not believe the breadth and width of some folks' imagination and inventiveness. Some are down right scary!

Even though 100% consensual most are 98% crazy, and I hope you enjoy every one.

Brad Tassell

You Did It Where?

1

At the foot of my parents' bed while they were asleep...

Pete

"Uh ...Harold, I think the dog has your shoes again."

2

On top
of
the Batmobile...

Kim

"Holy wax job, Batman!   Pow!!"

You Did It Where?

3

**On top of
the washer and dryer
in
the laundry room...**

Brad

"Is this the spin cycle, or do you always vibrate like that?"

4

Under the pew
in
church...

Al

"My friends, is that someone I
hear speaking in tongues?"

5

In the bank...

Colleen

"Collateral, I'll give you collateral!!"

6

**In the back seat
of my car;
my mother was in the
front and my brother
was driving...**

Joe

"When I said I wanted
grandchildren, I didn't mean
right this minute."

You Did It Where?

7

**I was on
the island of Malta,
in an
empty grave...**

Sam

"She was a little stiff at first."

8

**While bouncing
on a
trampoline...**

Cynthia

"Mrs. Johnson, you've just given birth to a bouncing baby boy."

9

In a treatment center for compulsive behavior...

Mike

"Three times! Hey, baby, I'm compulsive not bionic."

You Did It Where?

10

On a motorcycle going down San Pedro Ave. in San Antonio...

Holly

In these dangerous times I hope he wore his <u>little</u> helmet too.

11

**At Chuck E. Cheese
in
the mouse hole for
toddlers...**

Wes

You can slap, you can tickle,
you can flip your lid, get more
nookie than you ever did...

12

50 feet under water off the Cayman Islands...

Mike

"Yes darling, two minutes of air will be plenty."

13

On a pool table
in a
busy bar...

Carmen

What a classy broad.
Gee Carmen, can you say slut?

14

On a ski lift
in
Tahoe...

Ben

Just one piece of advice--
make sure to keep those tips up.

15

In my boss's chair...

Mike

"Marge, could you tell Mike to come in my office, please. What do you mean he already has?"

16

**In a morgue
in one
of the drawers...**

Sharron

"I said, stay still!"

17

The repair shop of a computer store...

Lori

"Would you like me to upgrade your floppy disk to a hard drive?"

18

On the floor of the deejay booth at a radio station...

Lynne

"I'd like to fill a request from Lynne. It's 'I Want Your Sex.' Everyone else, just listen to this song."

19

In
a downtown
phone booth...

Bart

"Citizens, I am in need of this phone booth."
"Don't worry Superman, Bart is as fast as a speeding bullet too."

You Did It Where?

20

In a Bethesda Navy Hospital bed with a third class Petty Officer...

Scott

"It's nice to see in your condition you're still able to salute."

21

Over the fry station
at
McDonalds...

Mike

Talk about your McNuggets!!

22

In a tanning bed...

Travis

Hey pal, that tan line looks like my sister!

23

In the trunk
of a
moving car...

Mur

"Guys, we're in the drive-in...
Guys? You can come out now."

24

On top
of a
cow trailer...

Stewart

"Your name wouldn't be Bessie, would it?"

25

In
a
grain bin...

Karen

"Oh, Billy Bob, the tractor ride, the possum stew, and now this. I must be the luckiest little filly in the world."

26

In a tree...

Marty

"When you all are done, could you bring down my cat?"

27

In a cornfield...

Tricia

Oh , yes !!

"Oh, baby, this is the best it's ever been!"
"Tricia, I'm over here?"

28

On a railroad bridge upside-down over a river...

Melissa

Just think of it as a really short bungee jump.

29

In a coal car...

R.

"Sweetie, stop a second, I think we've pressed a diamond."

30

**In
an
ice cream parlor...**

John

"I will only do that if you use the Fat Free Hot Fudge."

31

On
a
teeter-totter...

Tim

"You know, this would be much more fun if the other couple weighed the same as us."

32

On
an
airport runway...

Bruce

"Tower, this is flight two-niner from Sea-Tac. I think I just ran over a speed bump on your runway..."

33

In
a
prison waiting room...

Mike

"I know you have to smoke after sex dear, but we brought those cigarettes for my brother."

34

In a police car...

Patti

You have the right to remain silent. If you give up that right you may say, "Oh, Yes! Give it to me Copper!"

35

In the steam room, then the gym, and then the shower of the men's locker room during business

Kim

Now, that's what I call circuit training!!

36

The Australian exhibit of the world's fair...

Johnny

"Mommy, what are they doing?"
"Ah, that's the famous kangaroo
dance of Australia. Now, hurry,
let's go get a funnel cake."

37

While
we were
hang-gliding...

Cync

Yes, this is possible.
You just have to make sure
you're well hung.

38

In the courthouse with my husband, while my boyfriend was on trial for adultery...

Kristen

Are you sure you're not mixing your life up with last week's "All my Children?"

39

In a denture lab...

Mary

"Of course, you've made a good impression, but how will I explain all the teeth marks?"

40

**On top of
a traveling freight
train...**

Carrie

"I've been working on the
railroad. All the live long day."

41

On
a
soldering bench...

Scott

"Oh yes, honey, the IUD you made works just as good as my real one."

42

**Nov. 1989 Dresden,
East Germany,
in the rose bushes
in front of communist
headquarters...**

Mary

"Mary, your mission, should you decide to accept it, is to break the will of the last of the communist menace. This condom will self-destruct in five seconds."

43

The rear end
of a
snowmobile...

Jim

"Ever since we got rid of the sleigh, we can go around the world and still be to Grandma's house early."

44

In the library...

Mary

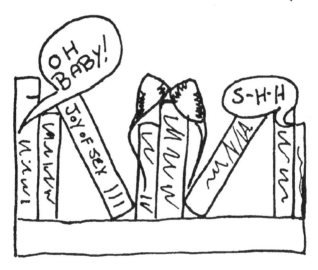

With Colonel Mustard and the candlestick, I'll bet.

45

Flying
in a
hot air balloon...

Mo

"Silly me, I thought by new
sexual heights you meant
orgasm!"

46

In
a
sewage pipe...

Pete

"Only the best for you, baby. Wanna wash those fries down with some Mad Dog 20/20?"

47

On the pedicure chair at the nail salon...

Justine

You're soaking in it!!

48

**On top
of
the town watertower...**

Henly

"Scientists are baffled by
residents reports of a strange
taste in the cities water supply.
One man remarked, 'It's kinda
familiar.' Film at eleven."

49

On an electric box in a generator field...

Denise

"If you were faking, why is your hair standing on end?"

50

In a big bowl of Jello...

Mike

"I don't want to ruin the mood, but did you know this stuff is made with ground horse hooves?"

You Did It Where?

51

**While riding
on a
jet ski...**

Marci

"You've gotta lean with me!"

52

Washington D.C. at the Lincoln Memorial in Lincoln's lap...

Chip

"Hurry up Honey, we're gonna be late for the theater."

53

On the Steps of the Washington Monument...

Chip

Had a busy week, huh Chip?

54

In an igloo...

Bill

"You said we were just gonna rub noses."
"Yes, but I didn't say what our noses would be rubbed on."

55

**In
my dentist's
chair...**

John

"Isn't this your fourth cleaning
this week?"

56

On a tour
of
Marengo Cave...

Debbie

"Now, if I'm on the top, are you a stalagmite or stalactite?"

You Did It Where?

57

**In the picture booth
at
the mall...**

Kari

"I'm sorry, Honey, the stool
doesn't spin that high."

58

In the boat going through "It's a Small World"...

Christie

You know **I** saw you doing it.
It **is** a small world after all.

You Did It Where?

59

**In
an
ambulance...**

Dan

"Quick get us to the drug store."
"Don't you mean the hospital?"
"No, drug store. She's not on the pill."

You Did It Where?

60

**The moving sidewalk
outside
Caeser's Palace...**
Keith

"I'll lay you 3 to 1 odds that
you're finished before we reach
the casino."

61

In a junk yard...

Frank

"Oh, Honey, growl like that
again.   I love it!"
"I thought that was you
growling?"

62

**In
the
funeral home...**

Kelle

"If you don't stop acting like you're not breathing, I'm getting out of here."

63

On the roof
of
Red Lobster...

Gregory

"Greg, you should have told me that I ordered the shrimp platter."

You Did It Where?

64

At the Experimental Aircraft Museum in Wisconsin...

Andrew

"And they said this plane would never get off the ground."

65

**The end zone
of
Shea Stadium...**

Frank

"Okay, Frank, it was good, but there's no reason to spike you condom."

You Did It Where?

66

In a baseball diamond dug out...

Jane

Talk about amazing!
Hit a home run and never left the
dug out.

67

On the roof
of an outhouse
in a
state park...

Shelly

"Hey, what's that smell?!"

68

In a B-52 bomber on top of a bomb...

Joanne

"Pilot to bomber-- Why haven't you dropped your load."
"We're trying!! We're Trying!!"

69

In
a
Texas mud hole...

Richard

"One more oink out of you, and I'm outta here!"

70

**In my race car,
in the pits,
during the race...**

Dale

"Twenty four seconds flat!
A new pit stop record."

You Did It Where?

71

On the log ride...

Dina

"I don't think I've ever been that wet!"

You Did It Where?

72

In the lawnmower section of K-mart...

Danny

"Attention K-Mart shoppers, we have a blue...Er...well, make that a red light special in the garden shop."

You Did It Where?

73

On
a
125 foot firetower...

James

"Do you smell smoke?"
"Forget it, I'm on my break."

74

On the rollercoaster....
Angie

"Keep your hands up!"

75

In the intake
of an
F-4 fighter jet...
Terry

"Roger, Red Leader. I've got smoke coming from the right engine, and it's not even running. Over."

76

On a bowling alley, starting on the foul line ending at the pins...

Joe

I don't care if you're naked or not, you're wearing those shoes.

77

In a kick boxing ring...

Kim

"All right slugger, work to the body, and keep her in a tight clinch, and you might go the distance."

You Did It Where?

78

**On top
of
the refrigerator...**

Don

Leftovers again!!!
I hope it wasn't a frigid-air.
Was it a top mount?

Hey, I know what your saying,
"Those sex places aren't very strange.
I'll show you strange."
Well, if you have a really strange place then send it in, and you could be in the next book. Or, if it's good enough, we'll do a whole book about you. Spend a little time and tell us about your place. Hell, slap the facts down on a couple of pages. If we use it we'll send you a copy of whatever we use it for. But remember you send it, we own it. And we won't give your address out or anything.
Send them to:

I DID IT THERE
LLESSAT PUBLISHING
527 N. GREENRIVER RD.
BOX 176
EVANSVILLE, IN 47711

Books by Brad Tassell include:

I'LL BE IN THE LOCKER, PORTRAITS OF A HIGH SCHOOL WUSS $5.95

HELL GIG, ENLIGHTENING THE ROAD COMIC $10.00

THE STRANGEST PLACES PEOPLE HAVE SEX $5.95

To order send check or money with $1.50 extra each for postage to:

LLESSAT PUBLISHING
527 N. GREENRIVER RD.
BOX 176
EVANSVILLE, IN 47711